Through Heaven and Back
Copyright © 2026 by Kristopher Perez

All rights reserved. No part of this book may be reproduced or transmitted in any form or by any means, electronic or mechanical, including photocopying, recording, or by any information storage and retrieval system, without prior written permission from the author, except in the case of brief quotations used in reviews or critical articles.

This is a work of poetry. Names, characters, and situations are the product of the author's imagination or used fictitiously. Any resemblance to actual events, locales, or persons, living or dead, is purely coincidental.

Cover and interior design by Kristopher Perez

Printed in the United States of America

First Paperback Edition

ISBN: 979-8-218-87062-1

for my lola here on earth and my lolo up in heaven

contents

part i : to the heavens

to the heavens	5
this is how the earth came to be	7
man	9
the beginning	11
the waters of donner	13
the sweetest conductor	15
my favorite color	17
you	19
beyond words	21
hold me	23
my heart	25
the end	27
i love you	29
a good morning	31
dreams of you	33
all to you	35
God dropped some diamonds	37

contents

part ii : a brief glance at the moon

when summer had begun	41
boy from jalisco	43
the sun and the moon	45
kiss	47
delicate behaviors	49
let it be so	51
your body	53
pure gold	55
the beauty of a blackbird	57
a brief glance at the moon	59
you become lonely	61
what is it that i must do?	63
ruin my peace	65
together	67
as pablo did	69
your desire for me	71

contents

part iii : the grief of losing

portraits of you	75
my mother's hands	77
feel again	79
the grief of losing	81
a king you shall be	83
shall i be envious?	85
woman	87
goodbye	89
to you, i apologize	91
may you find my love again	93
the mona lisa	95
what is this heartache?	97
five hundred	99
darling	101
look to the mountains	103
no better place	105
one	107

te amo sin saber cómo, ni cuándo, ni de dónde

(i love you without knowing how, or when, or from where)

pablo neruda

through heaven and back

part i

to the heavens

to the heavens

a key pressed from cosmic dust
fell through the altars of heaven
and into the divine seas where it formed,
and it was done perfectly.

then the key was lifted
atop the water's white foams
and was brushed to a shore of pebbled gold
where you knelt to retrieve its treasure
to fix betwixt thumb and finger
and polish it with your kiss.

and there my heart was,
cushioned within my chest over rare flowers
you picked from love's native soil,
when you turned the key
and set free these beams of light
shining far and above
and back to the heavens.

this is how the earth came to be

you looked at me
and mountains rose from flat ground,
and when you said my name for the first time,
your breath and mine formed the clouds
that sat at those mountain tops.

i said to you once that i wish i could lay
in the softness of your hair,
and so like a blanket, you drew lush grass
and perfect flowers over empty fields just for me.

all the times i called out for you,
your hands reached out for me,
your fingers stretching from the soil,
becoming the trees.

one time, your voice became a roar of thunder,
and so my tears made the rain,
and this made your eyes turn a deep brown
when you gave the color blue to the ground,
creating all of the seas and all of the oceans.

but, my darling, birds began to sing
when you took back my hands,
and the skies that were once a permanent gray,
turned bright with a perfect yellow center
from all the light that came from your beautiful smile.

this is how the earth came to be.

man

why is it so easy for me
to fall in love with you?

it is difficult to not love you
because what comes with not loving you
is the sky collapsing,
and the earth collapsing,
and there will be nothing,
and i will be nothing,
without you.

the beginning

i want time to pass so slow
that perhaps we could still be sipping
the hot broth from the first meal
we shared together the first time we met
with everything else waiting to unfold
that we've done together
since the beginning.

the waters of donner

the waters of donner
were extra blue for us that day,
and the horizon hid shyly behind
the mountains of pine trees.

you let me choose ground,
and once you knew i was happy,
you planted our tent into the earth
where we would house ourselves
for that one august afternoon.

in the water, i was frightful,
but you held me,
and you helped me
to find the calm in the lake.

but still,
this made you laugh,
and that made me laugh,
and so we laughed,
together,
in the waters of donner.

the sweetest conductor

when i hear your voice,
i hear an orchestra collected of the finest musicians
playing the most elite, most polished instruments,
performing a premier symphony just for me.

and there you are, the sweetest conductor,
conducting his orchestra with a pulse so succulent
that all i simply can hear is such sweet music
when i hear your voice.

my favorite color

you are my favorite color.

every shade of love you give
is my favorite color.

all the pigment,
bright and dim,
that comes from you,
is my favorite color.

a rainbow had never existed,
nor cannot exist,
nor does it exist,
nor will it ever exist,
because the most glorious color
exists only with me.

it's you.

you are my favorite color.

you

it's as if i had been handpicked by God
from seven billion people
to love the most precious of his creations.

you.

beyond words

i could sit here for a lifetime
and write all existing words
in every language onto my paper
and it would still not be enough
to proclaim my love for you.

hold me

my heart trembles when i feel your touch.

even your softest caress,
like delicate wind passing through the petals of a rose,
can submit me further into your loving grasp.

and that's just where i want to be.

so for as many moments as you'll allow, dear,
may you just hold me?

my heart

my heart belongs to you.

every untimely flutter and rhythmic throb
with each thrilling drumbeat
and unexpected burst of pitter-patter
belongs to you.

the end

i want time
to pass quickly
because i want
to see,
to live,
the future with you,
and i can't wait to know
that we did it all together
in the end.

i love you

i will never become capable
of creating a medley of words
all fixed to perfection
to declare my love for you.

only to you can i say
what has been said between other lovers
when centuries had witnessed
images that you and i only see in history books,
but never will those strangers
ever feel the weight of these words
as i do for you.

a good morning

it's you and me
lying together in between our bed sheets.

the early sunlight seeps through our blinds,
and the only sounds i hear are the melodic chirps
from the robins beyond our windows
and your faint breathing as you sleep here with me.

i want this to last forever,
so i ask,
to the heavens,
for just a minute more.

but then i hear
the tender shuffling
of footsteps
fast approaching
from down the hall
and into our room,
and before i know it,
she jumps into our bed,
and with such saccharine in her voice,
our little girl awakens us with,
"papa?"

dreams of you

what is it, dear,
that can make you dream of me?

do you dream of me
in the same ways i dream of you,
when, in the most inexplicable of ways,
the magnificence of what you are during the day
is replicated so vividly, so perfectly
within my eyes when they are closed at night?

oh, the beauty that you are in my dreams.

and even in the morning, when my eyes reopen,
do those dreams of you ensue.

all to you

if i were to send you a letter,
would you read it?

i'd write to you everyday.

the first thing i'd do,
as light first shines over God's horizon,
is place words in their perfect order,
as perfect as you, dear,
for only your eyes to see
before the sun falls back into the ocean.

if i write to you, my dear,
would you write back to me?

such an act it is
to place words born safely in one's heart
and force them to live on paper,
but for you, dear, i'll do just that.

and i'll continue,
oh, how i'll continue,
to seal all of my heartbeats
and enclose them all to you.

God dropped some diamonds

God dropped some diamonds
and they rested atop your shoulders
i held when we first danced.

God dropped some diamonds
and they rested atop your shoulders
i held when we last danced.

part ii

a brief glance at the moon

when summer had begun

summer hadn't begun
at the first sight of marigolds in our town.

summer had begun
at the first sight of your smile,
when your two lips bloomed in the moonlight
and fell upon my lips,
and suddenly,
i felt the warmth of the sun in your palms,
as you held me gently in place for all of your kisses,
my hands tucked somewhere near your chest,
your hands moved somewhere near my waist,
as we fell further into the backseat
of your two-door nissan.

that's when summer had begun.

boy from jalisco

boy from jalisco,
keep me warm
with your breath's whisper,
and with your native tongue,
show me all of your favorite ways
to say, "love."

the sun and the moon

the color hazel erupts around your pupils,
and as your darkened curls
keep your vision hidden in shadow,
i can still see the sun and the moon
dance in your eyes.

ask me what i'd want to do with you,
and i'll say, first, that i'd want to move
those darkened curls away from your eyes,
the same way your eyes have fixed
my heart back into place.

ask me what i'd want to do with you,
and i'll say, last, that i'd want to dance with you
the way the sun and the moon
dance in your eyes.

kiss

when i kiss you,
i kiss all of you.

your pinkened lips
that surround the words you speak
with some ease and much seduction,
your arms
that always pin me close to your heart,
your head
that carries your brain
that holds all the images of me
that you collect each of the nights
where i've begged so desperately to see you,
just so i can kiss you.

all of you.

delicate behaviors

such a small space is the backseat,
but how i love being here
because it's the only place
where you allow me to be close to you.

your stubble
against my cold fingertips.

goosebumps,
no space to breathe,
delicate behaviors with your soft lips.

let it be so

if my brain would only hold all of you,
having me forget everything that is not you,
i would let it be so.

your body

blood shoots in and out of my heart
when my fingertips brush your face,
and after my arms wrap around your muscled torso,
i position myself around your hardened waist
while the warming of your breath
passes through your moistened lips
and onto my neck and chest,
and then i look into your eyes,
your fingertips now brushing my face,
until both your hands draw my mouth in
to meet yours.

oh, how my body craves your body.

pure gold

the metal
of the ring
of your future lover
will not compare,
nor come closely
to the luster
of the precious green
and pure gold
trapped in your eyes.

the beauty of a blackbird

you find beauty
at the sight of a blackbird
as he flies with peace just outside
the frame of your room's window,
its golden-yellow crown,
more yellow, more captivating than the sun.

you smile when you see him
as he's perched on the branch of the tree
that, at times, obstructs your view of me
when i wait outside your window too.

you find beauty
when the blackbird sits in peace before you,
as if he arrived at this tree just for you,
to show love to you,
and you become so enamored
by how his wings can expand
in the same way my arms expand
just for you.

and once he goes away
and back into the sun's light,
oh, how i wonder,
if you think of him again and hope for his return,
or, beautiful boy,
is it just in those moments,
only when he is with you,
that you are so enamored?

a brief glance at the moon

let me stay enfolded in your arms,
and together our breathing can become one,
and as you hold me,
we can take a brief glance at the moon.

boy of wheat-colored skin,
if i may ask,
do you think the moon has witnessed
all the times we've tried to hide from its light?

even though the moon
will never know our names,
i will still kiss you under its light,
so that perhaps when your name and my name
no longer share the same space,
any night you have the chance
to take a brief glance at the moon,
you'll have a brief chance
to remember my name.

you become lonely

when your hands are empty,
and without a drink,
and without an invitation
into a crowded room
full of beautiful boys just like you,
who you want to like you,
and dance with you,
and make temporary love with you,
you reach out for me,
because i like you,
and i'd dance with you,
and make permanent love with you.

and even though
my eyes are the last set of eyes
you yearn to look into every night,
they still look out for you,
and even if they cry because of you,
they remain open for you
whenever you become lonely.

what is it that i must do?

what is it that i must do
in order to be trapped
in your arms once again?

to be within your space,
please tell me
what it is that i must do?

to be the one you dream of,
to be the one you desire,
to be the one you love,
i would commit to it, beautiful boy.

please just tell me
what it is that i must do?

ruin my peace

please.

i'm on my hands and knees.

for why would i work endlessly
to craft something i'd want indestructible
if it were that i did not want it tested,
if it were that i did not want your weight
to rattle me,
to fall into me,
to come onto me,
like a boulder dropping deeply into still water?

how can i know my peace is truly stable
if i don't give you a moment to try and destroy it?

please.

i'm on my hands and knees.

together

many times we have occupied
the same space together.

your skin, woven perfectly
from the stories of your ancestors
whose stories remain rooted
somewhere deep in guadalajara.

my skin, wrapping perfectly my tired bones
that frame and protect my own frail heart
passed down to me from the love
shared between my lolo and my lola.

many times, your skin and mine,
warmed us both,
all fibers of you and me,
from your head to my toes,
in the same space together.

and in an instant,
i now occupy that space alone.

and in an instant,
nothing will occupy that space,
that we once did,
together.

as pablo did

from my shelf into your hands
are neruda poems,
words i'd read repeatedly
the last ten years,
bound with pages almost yellowed,
traveling miles with me for comfort,
existing in regions where languages spoken
are different from where i call home,
existing as a resource just for me
to hold in my own hands,
to see with my own eyes,
for that one day i could write
to express all my love and desire,
just as pablo did,
for someone like you.

from my life into your hands
are those neruda poems.

your desire for me

for as long as summer had lasted,
so, too, did your desire for me.

as quickly as how the warmth of the sun
changed into the brisk air that now carries
the browned and sorbet flora
from your part of town
to my part of town,
so, too, did your desire for me.

for as long as 129 days,
from june to october,
you wanted me,
and i, too, wanted you,
but now that the season has changed,
so, too, did your desire for me.

part iii

the grief of losing

portraits of you

in my head, dear, you will remain.

as fast as how the light steals the dark
from within your bedroom walls
to sweetly signal you to awaken,
and to fall back into my arms
before the dark returns,
as do sweet thoughts of you,
bearing like fruit,
come into my head,
and there they will remain.

i've witnessed your beautiful face,
your hair, dark with hints of the moon's light,
such as the sky was when we first met,
more times than i've witnessed
your beautiful face in my real little life.

and all of those portraits of you,
as certain as how the dark steals the light
from my little life when you are nowhere near me,
in my head, dear, they will remain.

my mother's hands

my mother caught my tears in her hands,
as if God created her beautiful palms
just for this moment.

my mother's hair,
dark such as her own father's,
graceful such as her own mother's,
fell onto my face and covered my tired eyes
as i cried for you.

because of you, tears fell quickly,
and from my heart they poured,
such as my heart did with love for you.

but because of my mother,
my dear, beautiful mother,
my tears never found their way to the ground
the same way harsh drops of rain
find their way to the soil
as my mother caught my tears instead,
safely, right in her beautiful palms,
safely, right in her beautiful hands.

feel again

i don't want to see you again
because i don't want you to leave again.

the moment after we had last touched
came a feeling i no longer want to feel again.

the grief of losing

how can it be
that i feel so strongly
the grief of losing you?

should i not have felt
the joy of loving you
just as strongly?

how can it be
that the handful of times
our chests were pressed closely together
enough that the separate tugging of our hearts
felt like one,

how can it be
that i did not feel love for you then,
but i feel it now instead?

oh, how i feel it now.

a king you shall be

to me, a king you shall be,
and for you, i shall put everything first
ahead of myself,
beyond what my head knows
is right or wrong,
beyond what my heart feels
is right or wrong,
without any concern,
without any second thought,
without a third or fourth thought,
and even if by doing so meant
you would never make me one in return,
for even if it meant it could destroy me,
and everything around me,
and everything that is me,
to me, a king you shall still be.

shall i be envious?

shall i be envious of his ways,
in which one of them,
his hand can so easily rest on your chest?

shall i be envious
that he can ignite your heart so quickly,
so unbelievably,
as if together you both had discovered fire,
and so you wrap your arms around him
the same way your arms once wrapped around me?

his hand lay on your chest,
and against his palm,
your heart taps the same taps that i once felt
when i would lay my head on your chest.

but now, you make his heart tap.

shall i be envious?

woman

strawberry lotion sweetly veils
her delicate fingers,
and once they are silken,
she touches your rough body,
and so you tell her that it feels perfect
and that she is perfect.

the veins that pulse underneath
her warm wheat skin
remind you of roads on a map,
and so you trace them
with your rough touch
until you are just as soft as she is.

your favorite shade of your favorite color
is painted on her lips tonight,
and so you kiss her,
and i can almost taste what she tastes
from kissing you too.

and now, both you and the wind
exchange a dance with her,
and while she holds you,
my hands yearn to do
all that her hands do with you.

goodbye

if, for now, i tell you, "goodbye,"
how long would God have me wait
until he'd let me greet you again?

if i were to say, "goodbye,"
would you fight for me to take it back
or would you so easily say, "goodbye," too?

dear boy,
this long silence you always give me,
such is the distance between me and the moon,
makes me think it may be best
to just take one last look at your face,
your face that has always captivated me
and arrested me with its beauty,
and just say to you,
 "goodbye."

to you, i apologize

to you, i apologize
for being more
than what your desires were.

to you,
beautiful boy,
i gave my all,
and i apologize
that your arms were not created
to hold the weight of the adoration
i had for you.

beautiful boy,
to you, i apologize,
that the ground on which you stand
could not withstand the magnitude
of my admiration for you,
of my deep fondness of you,
the enormity of all this endearment
i had for you.

and to you, beautiful boy,
i apologize, truly,
on behalf of everything in your life
that keeps you from welcoming
all of my love into your life
and all the blessings that would follow.

may you find my love again

i hope perhaps you'll find my love again.

and even if it's not with me
but with someone other than me,
i hope you'll see that all the reasons
it feels like peace with him now
is because i was the first
to allow you to feel such love,
only for you to abandon this love,
to miss this love,
to crave this love,
to cry for this love,
to seek this love,
so that one day,
you may find peace again,
and so that one day,
you may find my love again.

the mona lisa

within moments, i took your heart,
and i made it larger than my own heart,
and suddenly,
you became the most beautiful being of all.

someone whose hands i formed myself
to hold with my own hands,
someone whose body i formed
to lay with my own restless body,
someone whose mouth i formed
to speak of sweet love just with me,
someone whose eyes i formed
to look into safely with my own eyes.

such as the beauty of a painting,
such as leonardo creating the mona lisa
with only a brush in hand,
thanks to me, here you exist.

what is this heartache?

why is it my heart's desire
for the air to brush through its chambers,
for the light to reach deep into its cavities?

my cry for love has moved the same distance
only the sun has ever traveled,
but my tears will never be recognized
as they swell, instead, only within my chest.

five hundred

i will wait for you,
and if i must,
i will wait in line with hundreds of others.

be they men who find sensation
in your favorite bouteille de vin,
be they women whose hips dance
as exquisitely as the fabric wrapped around them,
i will wait for you.

and even if i shall be
the five hundredth person,
the last in line with whom you come to fall in love,
i will promise to prove to you, my dear,
just why there was no other person
in line after me.

darling

so many times i have seen you
through day and through night,
but today i see you
through blue and through gold
all around this chapel.

like how the stars dance around the planets,
these colors dance around us both,
and in all the languages that exist,
in none of them can i express this warmth.

my darling, become my everything,
as you are the only man i shall love,
and my eyes will only ever hold your light
even after the sun has set on today.

for how many years did it take this chapel's walls
to fall together and encase our love?

the light of your darling face,
the beauty that is your name,
my dear stripling,
let these façades see you kiss me.

they are ready, as am i.

look to the mountains

i'd call to every person,
from the mountains,
and announce my love for you,
how immense this romance is
that i feel for you,
and the greatness of my speech
shall move the entire region,
and they shall look up at me
in wonderment and in question,

"is this what love can do and has done?"

"how could God allow any person
to behave in such a way?"

"look to the mountains!
oh, what love has done to this poor man."

no better place

what if there is no better place
after my body is burnt
to resemble the sands of a shore?

after i declare my love for you
for the last time,
what if there is no better place
for me to wait until you're sand too,
where we can hold again,
and kiss again,
and love again?

why not let me hold you now,
and kiss you now,
and love you now,
if there is no better place?

one

what are the chances that you came to be?

the remnants of the stars that surround
such unfamiliar space had collected together
to compose something with such brilliance
to bring a new brightness into my own world.

or it might have been from the hands of God,
because i thought he could not exist,
as he sat down and brought you together
from the most blessed and beautiful
of his surroundings in heaven,
finding which parts fit perfectly with the next,
like a puzzle until it was complete for him
to introduce you to me
and convince me
he is real.

Kristopher Perez was born and raised in Reno, Nevada. His roots trace back to the Philippines, where his grandparents met across a divide of class and circumstance - his lolo, whose hands bore the weight of labor, and his lola, raised in comfort and grace as the daughter of an army officer.

Raised by his mother, Lilian, alongside his siblings Kristine, Angelo, and Jacob, Perez grew up in a home shaped by imagination, humor, and unwavering devotion. Afternoons spent with his mother in early childhood watching *I Love Lucy* reruns first awakened his love for performance and storytelling. That early fascination blossomed into a deep appreciation for acting, theatre, cinema, music, and writing - art forms that would shape his creative world and his sense of emotional expression.

His passion for performance eventually led him to acting in plays, and later to formal training at the Ruskin School of Acting.

Through Heaven and Back is Perez's debut collection of poetry.

Made in the USA
Coppell, TX
24 February 2026